THE CZECH BOOK

by Irene Tognazzini Turk

and

N.C. Tognazzini

DOGGEREL™
P R E S S

an imprint of ENERGEIA™ PUBLISHING, Inc.
Salem, Oregon U.S.A.

ISBN: 0-9626591-0-X

Library of Congress Catalog Card Number: 90-81718

May 1990

The authors and publisher of this book in no way wish to offend Czechoslovakia or the Czech people.

Illustrated by Irene Tognazzini Turk.

To Dad

DEFINITION

check (chek) Czech (chek) n. a stop; a restraint; a mark placed against items in a list; a pattern of squares in cloth; a short hairy man wearing a furry hat, peacoat and clumpy boots ... etc. ...

THIS IS A CZECH

THIS IS NOT A CZECH

CZECHERS

RAIN CZECH

TRAVELER'S CZECH

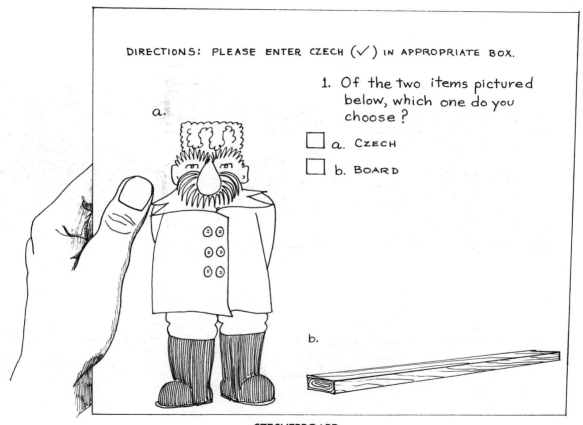

CZECHERBOARD

COURT CZECHSTER

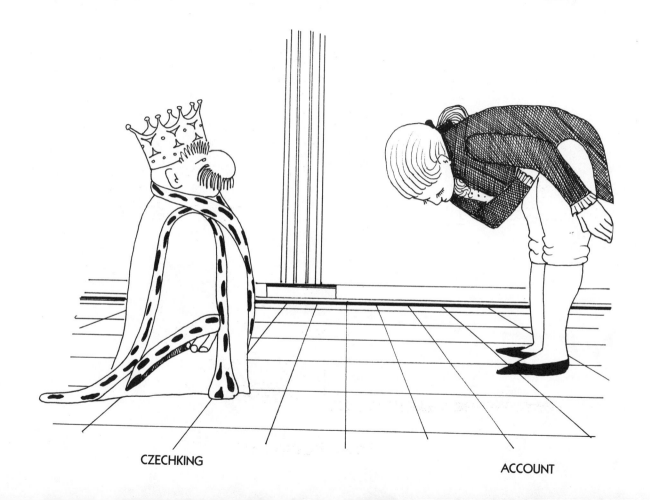

CZECHKING   ACCOUNT

CZECH AND SEE

CZECHXICAN

MAY I HAVE MY CZECH PLEASE?

CZECHASS

CASHING A CZECH

HAT CZECH

OVERDRAWN CZECH

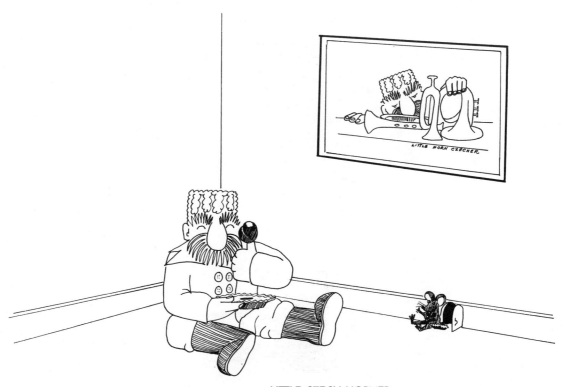

LITTLE CZECH HORNER

MICHAEL CZECHSON

CZECH AND JILL

CZECHXCITED

COMPANY CZECH

WILLIAM CZECHSPEARE

CORN CZECHS

JOHN STEINCZECH

FLIGHT CZECH

DATING A CZECH

POST-DATING A CZECH

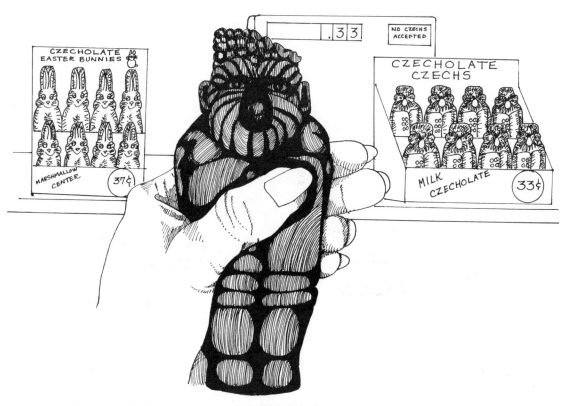

CZECHOLATE

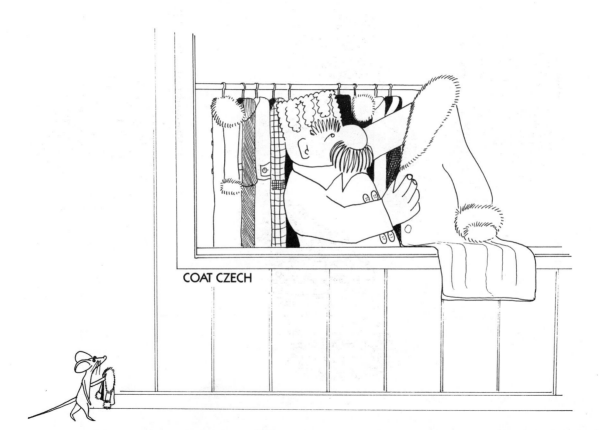

COAT CZECH

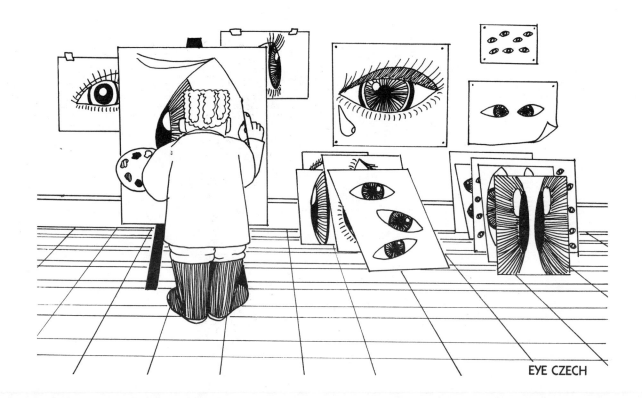

EYE CZECH

CZECH STUB

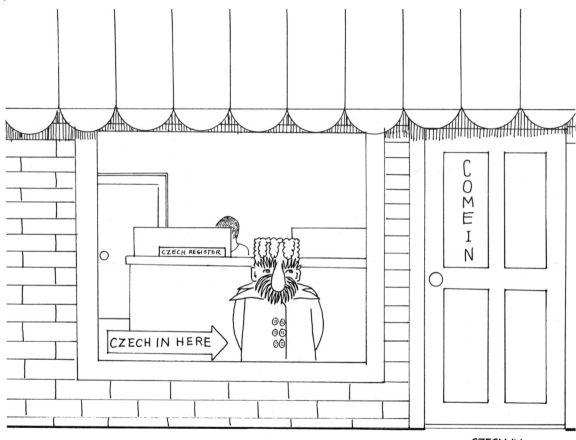

CZECH OUT

CZECH OF ARABY

LIKE A CZECHEN WITH ITS HEAD CUT OFF

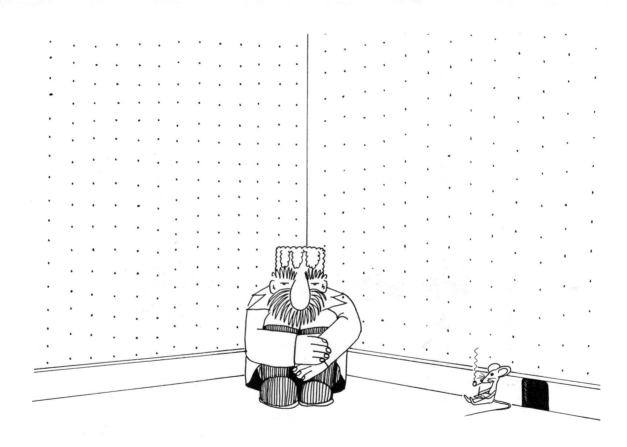

CZECH WITHDRAWAL

CZECH ON THE PATIENT

CZECHMONK

DANCING CZECH TO CZECH

CZECHY ONASSIS

CZECH-IN-THE-BOX

EATING CZECHS CEREAL

CZECHERS THE CLOWN

STOLEN CZECH

CZECH BE NIMBLE

CZECH BENNY

CZECH THE RIPPER

CZECH MARKS

CZECHSAW PUZZLE

BLANK CZECH

LARGE CZECH

NO CZECHS ACCEPTED

CZECHEN LIVERS

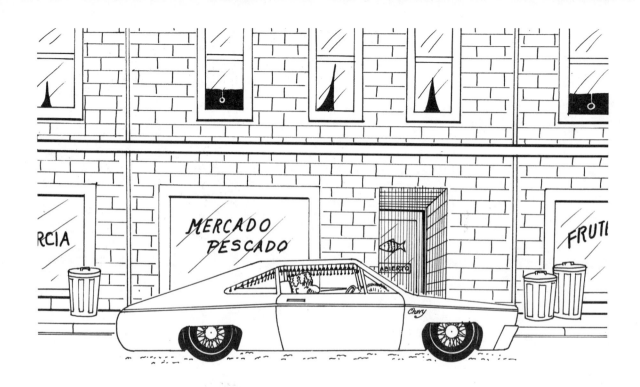

CZECHANO

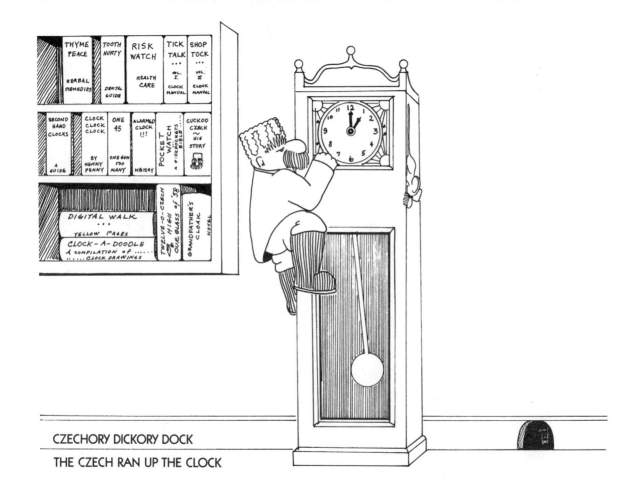

CZECHORY DICKORY DOCK

THE CZECH RAN UP THE CLOCK

SIGNED CZECH

COUNT CZECHULA

REV. JESSE CZECHSON

NEW CZECHXICO

CZECH-O-LANTERN

CHECHXAS CHAINSAW MASSACRE

CZECHED TABLECLOTH

CZECHEN COOP

CZECH ON THE BABY

STOPPING A CZECH

CZECHXICAN JUMPING BEAN

PASSING A BAD CZECH

THE CZECH IS IN THE MAIL

RICE CZECHS

CZECH POINT

WHEAT CZECHS

EAR CZECH

CUTTING A CZECH

BANK
of
LONDON

CZECH ON A FOREIGN BANK

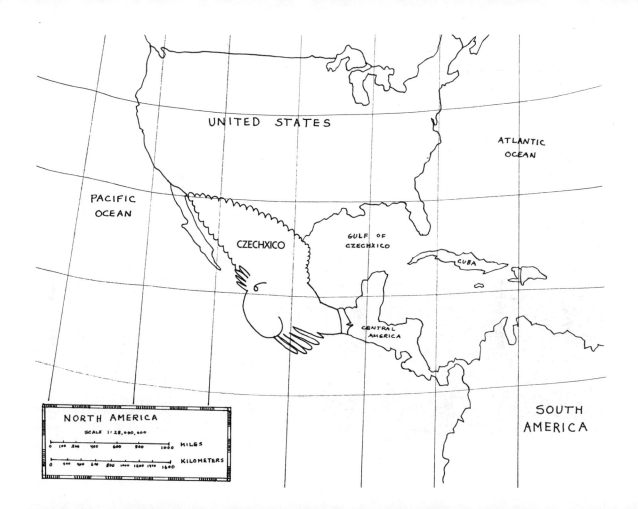

UNITED STATES

ATLANTIC
OCEAN

PACIFIC
OCEAN

CZECHXICO

GULF OF
CZECHXICO

CUBA

CENTRAL
AMERICA

SOUTH
AMERICA

NORTH AMERICA

SCALE 1:28,000,000

0   100   200   400   600   800   1000   MILES

0   200   400   600   800   1000   1200   1400   1600   KILOMETERS

CZECHENPOX

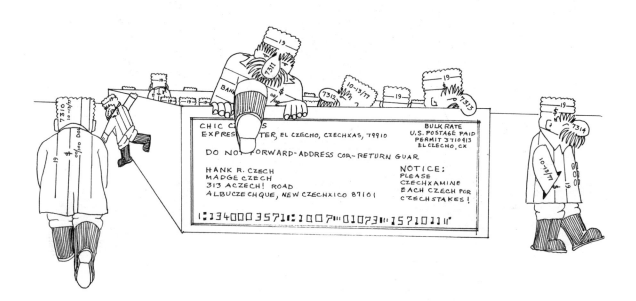

BOX OF PREPRINTED CZECHS

CZECH RABBIT

CZECH COOK AND BOTTLE WASHER

CZECHERED PAST

CHEST CZECHX-RAY

CZECHSI

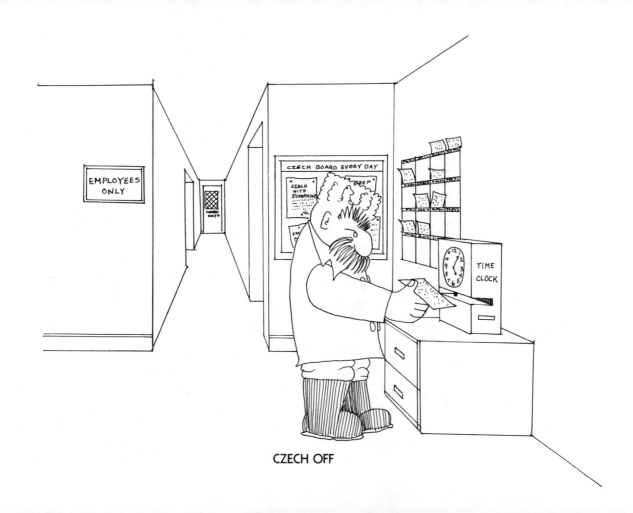

CZECH OFF

PLAYING CZECHS

MACZECH

CZECH OFF THE OLD BLOCK

CZECHUP